Ashton Oxenden

Prayers for Private Use

Ashton Oxenden

Prayers for Private Use

ISBN/EAN: 9783744747660

Printed in Europe, USA, Canada, Australia, Japan

Cover: Foto ©Lupo / pixelio.de

More available books at **www.hansebooks.com**

Prayers for Private Use.

BY THE.

REV. ASHTON OXENDEN,

**RECTOR OF PLUCKLEY, KENT,
AND HONORARY CANON OF CANTERBURY.**

THIRTY-EIGHTH THOUSAND.

LONDON:

HATCHARD AND CO. PICCADILLY, W.

WILLIAM MACINTOSH, PATERNOSTER ROW.

———

1868.

CONTENTS.

OUR Father, Which art in heaven, Hallowed be Thy Name. Thy kingdom come. Thy will be done in earth, as it is in heaven. Give us this day our daily bread. And forgive us our trespasses, as we forgive them that trespass against us. And lead us not into temptation ; but deliver us from evil : For Thine is the kingdom, the power, and the glory, for ever and ever. Amen.

Sunday Morning.

O ALMIGHTY and Merciful Father, look down from heaven and hear me, as I approach Thee on the morning of Thine own day.

Thanks be unto Thee for having spared me to the beginning of it. Pardon me for not having profited so much as I ought by those which are past. O forgive me, for Christ's sake, for having wasted the precious hours which might have brought so many blessings to my soul.

And now, Lord, help me to live this day as one who is earnestly seeking heaven. Draw away my thoughts from the things of the world, and enable me to fix them upon Thee. Come Thou, and dwell in my heart.

B

Drive out every intruder, and take full possession Thyself. Make this the best and happiest day that I have ever spent.

Give me a serious and thoughtful frame of mind; and prepare me for all those sacred ordinances in which I am about to engage. Bless them abundantly to my soul, and give me much enjoyment in them. Tune my heart for Thy service. Fit me for the blessed work of prayer and praise. Hast Thou not promised, Lord, that where two or three are gathered together in Thy name Thou Thyself wilt be in the midst of them? Fulfil that promise to me. Meet me in the courts of Thy house, and pour out upon me a spirit of true and earnest devotion. And when Thy word is read, or preached, grant that I may listen with a humble and believing heart. Bring home some precious truth today to my soul. Break this hard heart of mine, and make it feel. Speak, Lord, to my conscience. May Thy gospel come to me, not in word only, but also in power.

Bless my beloved brethren. May Thy

courts be thronged with devout worshippers. O my God, on this day of peace and rest visit the world with Thy mercy, and save the lost.

Holy Father, I pray to Thee for Thy servants who are about to minister before Thee. Prepare them for their heavenly work. Teach them by Thy Holy Spirit, that they may teach others ; and whilst they sow the seed of life, make their own souls to be as a watered garden. Bless especially the minister of this parish. Lift up his hands, I beseech Thee ; cheer his heart ; and prosper him in his work.

And now, O my Father, I commend myself into Thy hands. Be with me during every hour of this holy day. Open the windows of heaven, and pour down a large blessing upon me, not according to the measure of my worthiness, but according to the abundant riches of Thy grace, and for the sake of Jesus Christ, our Lord. Amen.

Our Father, &c

Sunday Evening.

MOST gracious God, I come to Thee this night to ask Thee to pardon my sins, and to thank Thee for Thy many blessings.

When I look back on the hours that are past, I feel that I have much reason to humble myself before Thee. My heart has gone astray. My thoughts have wandered. The world has crept in, and spoilt my devotions. What coldness, and dulness, and unbelief, hast Thou seen in me! O pity me, and forgive me, for my Redeemer's sake. Blot out every sin, and especially the sin of my prayers and devotions. Wash me in the blood of the Lamb, and I shall be whiter than snow.

Come to me now, my Saviour, and speak peace to my soul. Take me, sinful as I am,

and make me Thine. Subdue my stubborn
will. Fix my wayward heart. O Thou Sun
of Righteousness, shine upon my soul this
night. And before I go to rest, make me to
feel that all is well with me, that I am Thy
servant, and that Thou art my Surety, my
Friend, my daily and hourly Portion.

Accept the many prayers which have this
day been offered up by Thy people throughout
the world. Accept mine, poor and feeble as
they have been, and mixed with so much sin.
Bless the word that has been preached. Make
it a word of life to many, and especially to
myself. Comfort the mourning; enlighten
the ignorant ; turn into the right way those
who have wandered from it. Convert the
sinful. Lead on those in whom Thou hast
begun a good work. Save them by Thy
almighty grace.

Grant a blessing to my own parish and
neighbourhood. Help me to do some good in
my station. Make me in some degree useful to
others. And grant that each day I may desire
to glorify Thee, and to serve Thee faithfully.

I thank Thee for every past mercy, especially for the many rich blessings, which I have this day enjoyed. Make me, I beseech Thee, a holier, a better, and a happier Christian. May I live upon Christ now, and be ever looking forward to His second coming. Fit me for a never-ending sabbath in Thy courts above; and grant that I may hereafter enjoy that eternal rest, which remaineth for Thy people in heaven.

Hear me in this and all my prayers, for Jesus Christ's sake. Amen.

Our Father, &c.

Monday Morning.

LOOK down from heaven, O my God, and hearken to the prayer of Thy unworthy servant. My wants are great; but, Lord, Thy power to relieve is greater. Thou art the very Fountain: I come to Thee poor and needy; O fill me out of Thy fulness. Thou delightest to give; send me not empty away.

Lord, I thank Thee for all Thy past mercies to my body and my soul. I thank Thee for the measure of health which I enjoy, for the food which I eat, for the clothing which I put on, for the home in which I dwell. I thank Thee for the kind and dear friends who care for me, for the portion which Thy love allots to me in this world, for Thy great kindness in watching over me, for shielding me from a thousand dangers, and for sparing my life up to this hour.

But still more I bless Thee for Thy spiritual gifts. How great is Thy love to my soul! Thou hast given me a Saviour to die for me. Thou hast pointed out the way by which a lost one may be saved. O Jesus, save me.- Sprinkle Thy own blood upon my soul. Stretch out the arms of Thy mercy, and receive me, sinner as I am. O give me the joy of acceptance, the blessedness of pardon. Say to me, gracious Lord, thy sins be forgiven thee. And make me Thine for ever, Thy true servant, Thy faithful follower, Thy loving disciple.

O my God, enable me this day to live nearer to Thee than I have yet done. Strengthen my faith; increase my love; fill me with Thyself; draw my sinful heart towards Thee.

Lord, I desire to know all the evil that is in me. Show me to myself I beseech Thee. Show me the hatefulness of my guilt; and make me to abhor myself, and repent in dust and ashes. Thou hast called me unto holiness ;

sanctify me by Thy blessed Spirit. Lead me, O lead me, in the narrow path of life. Enable me to break off every evil habit, especially ——. And if there is any hidden sin lurking in my heart, give me grace to overcome it.

May the blessedness of Thy own day still rest upon me. Let me not forget those holy lessons which were taught me in Thy house. Deepen any good impression which has been made. Carry on any work of grace which Thou Thyself hast begun in me. Make my future course a useful and a happy one. Make me a blessing to others. Lord, I have been too much a cumberer of the ground. Grant that I may now bear fruit. Show me what Thou wouldst have me to do, and give me grace to do it.

Bless my minister, and those whom Thou hast committed to his care. Help him to sow the seed of life; and may it spring up in many hearts. The harvest is truly plenteous; send faithful labourers to gather souls into Thy garner.

Be with those especially who are gone forth
to labour in distant lands. O Lord, prosper
them in their arduous work ; and as they bear
the burden and heat of the day, may their own
souls be refreshed, and may they receive a
full reward.

Hear me, O my Father ; and give me all
that I have asked, and all that I need, for my
Saviour's sake. Amen.

Our Father, &c

Monday Evening.

O THOU who art not only my God, but also my Father, I thank Thee that Thou dost encourage me to draw near to Thee as Thy child. O give me a Father's blessing.

Thou art acquainted with all my wants. Every trial, every sorrow, every craving of my heart, is known to Thee. I am weak; do Thou strengthen me. I am poor; do Thou enrich me. I come to Thee in all my emptiness; do Thou fill me out of Thy fulness. Give me all that I need, and more than I dare to ask. Give me, not according to my worthiness, but according to my necessity, and according to the abounding riches of Thy grace.

And, O God, Thou knowest likewise all my

sins. Make *me* to know them also, and to feel their greatness. Call to my remembrance all that is past. Show me where I have been wrong. Bring to light my hidden iniquities. I acknowledge the guilt of my evil thoughts, my unholy desires, my secret transgressions. Pardon me, O my Father, for Jesus' sake. Blot out my sins in that precious blood which was shed for me on the cross. Take away this heart of stone, and give me a heart of flesh — a tender, believing, loving heart.

O Lord, help me to live nearer to Thee day by day. Keep me under the blessed influence of Thy Holy Spirit. Make me to be constantly growing in grace. Forgetting those things which are behind, may I be ever pressing towards the prize of my high calling. Give me grace to crucify self, to keep under my body, and to bring my thoughts and desires and will into subjection to Thee.

Take me, O my God, under Thy gracious care this night. Refresh me with sleep and rest. Let Thy fatherly hand ever be over me. Let Thy Holy Spirit ever be with me. Make me to feel safe and happy under Thy protection.

Bless, O Lord, those who are near and dear to me. Give unto them all that I have asked for myself. If any of them are at this time in sorrow, do Thou comfort them. If in doubt or difficulty, do Thou guide them. Those of them who are still afar off from Thee, do Thou bring near. And to those who know and love Thee, give more and more of Thy grace.

Hear me, O my Father; and give me an answer of peace to these my prayers, for Jesus Christ's sake. Amen.

Our Father, &c.

Tuesday Morning.

O ALMIGHTY FATHER, through Thy mercy I am spared to begin another day. Thanks be unto Thee for Thy safe keeping during the past night, for watching over me during the hours when I was helpless, and for defending me from the many dangers which might have hurt me.

O Thou God of love, make me to feel that Thou lovest *me*. O my Saviour, who art willing to gather me under Thy wings, draw me to Thyself. I thank Thee, I praise Thee, I adore Thee for Thy great goodness. Glory be to Thee for all that Thou art in Thyself, and all that Thou hast done for me. Give me a thankful heart now ; and grant that I may praise Thee hereafter in Thy courts above.

O Lord, I earnestly desire to be holy. Help me to attain to a higher state in the Christian life. Enable me to walk in the narrow path which leads to heaven. Give me Thy Holy Spirit to dwell within me. Take away from me the love of sin, and stamp Thine own image upon my soul.

I confess that this present world has too strong a hold of me. I am tied and bound by its chains. O loose me from them and set me free. May my heart and my hope be in heaven. May I feel that Thou art my portion, and my exceeding great reward.

Heavenly Father, be with me this day. Keep me near to Thee, and uphold me every moment lest I fall. Let me engage in nothing which is contrary to Thy will. Show me what Thou wouldest have me to do, and where Thou wouldest have me to go. I have lived too long to myself; I desire henceforth to live to Thee : O enable me to do so. Bless me in all my ways, and make me a blessing to others. Enable me to do some good this day ; and in all I say or do give me a single eye to Thy glory. Make me very watchful over my thoughts. Preserve me from all unholy desires. Subdue my unruly will, and bring it into subjection to Thy will. Make me watchful over my thoughts and words. Keep Thou the door of my lips, that I offend not with my tongue.

And since I know not what a day may bring forth, do Thou order every event of my future life. Mark out my course for me. If prosperity be my portion, make me thankful, and keep me humble. Or if trials and sorrows come upon me, let me receive them as from Thee; and may they all work together for my eternal good. Whatever Thou art pleased to give me, let me never forget Thee, the great and gracious Giver ; and whatever Thou takest from me, O be Thou still with me.

I now commit myself into Thy hands. Do for me as Thou seest best. Only save my precious soul, and make me Thine for ever. All that I ask is in the name of Jesus Christ, my Lord. Amen.

Our Father, &c.

Tuesday Evening.

O MY God, I heartily thank Thee for the mercies I am continually receiving, and for all Thy goodness to my body and my soul. Thou hast been very gracious in preserving me in health, and shielding me from danger. Thine eye has followed me, and Thou hast marked out my path. O be with me still. I feel that I want Thy guidance and direction in all I do. Let Thy wisdom counsel me, Thy hand lead me, and Thine arm support me.

If I have been kept from sin this day, or strengthened to resist the tempter, to Thee be all the praise. And if I have been enabled to do anything rightly, glory be to Thee for that grace which has been so mercifully given to me.

Lord, I put myself into Thy hands. Help me to correct all my evil ways. Keep me close to Thee. Give me more and more grace. Fill me with Thy Holy Spirit. Make Christ very precious to my soul. May I lean upon Him day by day, and trust Him with a simple faith.

Breathe into my soul, O God, holy and heavenly desires. Give me a clean heart, and renew a right spirit within me. Conform me to Thine own image. Make me like my Saviour. O that I may both look to Him as my atoning sacrifice, and also daily endeavour to follow the steps of His most holy life! Enable me in some measure to live here on earth as He lived, and to act in all things as He would have acted.

Lord, as Thou hast been about my path this day, so be Thou about my bed this night. And when I presently lie down to rest, give me gentle and refreshing sleep, and a calm and settled peace. And when at length I lie down to rise no more, may I sleep in Jesus, and wake up in His likeness.

Grant that I may profit by what I have read from Thy holy word. I thank Thee for all the means of grace which I enjoy. Teach me Thine own self, and lead me into the knowledge and love of Thy truth.

Be with my dear relations. Make them very dear to Thee. And if any of them are still afar off, O bring them home, gracious Lord, to Thy fold. Bless my intercourse with them, and help me to try and do them good.

Hear me, O my Father, and accept my unworthy offering of prayer and praise, for Jesus Christ's sake. Amen.

Our Father, &c.

Wednesday Morning.

O GOD, who didst at the first command the light to shine out·of darkness, I thank Thee for having brought me to the beginning of another day. I praise Thee for this, and for all Thy other mercies. Let me never forget that my very life hangs upon Thy goodness, and that in Thee I live, and move, and have my being.

But, O Lord, there is something better than these temporal mercies, for which I have reason to bless Thee. Thou hast been very gracious to my soul. Thanks be unto Thee for having redeemed me through the blood of Thy dear Son. Thanks be unto Thee, O Saviour, for having given Thy life for me.

Enable me, in some measure, to love Thee

in return. Warm my cold heart, I beseech Thee. Take away all that hinders me from giving myself to Thee.

Holy Father, mould me according to Thine own image. Bend my will to Thine. Give me grace to obey Thee in all things, and ever to follow Thy gracious leading. Show me the way in which Thou wouldest have me to go, and enable me to walk in it, ever trusting Thee, and simply leaning on Thy strength.

Send down Thy Holy Spirit into my heart, to subdue my carnal affections, and to bring them into obedience to Thee. Let not the world have dominion over me, but enable me to live above it. Raise my thoughts heavenwards; and teach me day by day to live a life of faith, and to walk through this world as seeing Him who is invisible.

Lord, make me this day to be kind to my fellow-men, to be gentle and unselfish, careful to hurt no one by word or deed, but anxious to do good to all, and to make others happy. Give me a heart to feel for my brethren. Enable me to take au interest in their welfare, to rejoice in the prosperity of the prosperous, and to feel for the afflictions of the afflicted.

O Lord, forgive the sins of my temper. Pardon all my hasty words and unchristian thoughts. Make me watchful, that I offend not with my tongue. Give me a meek and loving spirit, which is in Thy sight of great price. Enable me, under every circumstance, to feel and act as becomes the follower of a holy Saviour.

O my Father, I would not live unto myself, but unto Thee. Help me so to live. Keep me from sin this day, and from all that may offend Thee. Watch over me, a poor, erring creature. Hold Thou me up, and I shall be safe. Keep me under Thy sheltering care, and never leave me until Thou hast brought me into Thy very presence, where I shall be safe for ever.

O God, supply all my wants, and accept my hearty thanksgiving, for Jesus Christ's sake. Amen.

Our Father, &c.

Wednesday Evening.

UNTO Thee, O Lord, do I lift up my soul.
Help me to draw near, not with my lips
only, but with my heart also. Pardon the
many unworthy offerings I have made Thee,
and all my prayers which have been so mixed
with sin. Forgive the imperfection even of
my best services, and accept me now in Christ
my Saviour.

O Jesus, I flee unto Thee to hide me. I
shelter myself under Thy righteousness. I
plead Thy merits, and trust to Thy all-
prevailing intercession. Undertake my cause,
I beseech Thee.

O blessed Spirit, Thou hast promised to
help my infirmities. Teach me how and what
to ask. Give me a devout mind ; and grant

that I may feel prayer to be not only a duty, but a delight.

Another day of mercy has passed away : O grant that I may have found peace through Christ. Another day of opportunity is gone : pardon its wasted and unimproved hours. Make me to remember that I am a day nearer to the joys of heaven, or to the miseries of hell. And since I shall soon lie down and die, make me ready for that time. Prepare me for it. I acknowledge with shame that I am too much taken up with the things of earth. The world and its occupations too deeply engross my thoughts and affections. Keep me mindful that the day of the Lord draweth nigh. Let my lamp be lighted. Make it to burn brightly. May I know the blessedness of that faithful servant who is ever waiting for his Lord's coming !

Shed abroad Thy love in my heart. Make me not only to fear Thee and obey Thee, but to love Thee above all my earthly friends. Enable me from my heart to say, Whom have I in heaven but Thee, and there is none upon earth that I desire in comparison with Thee.

Take me now under Thy protecting care. O my Father, watch over Thy child. Give me this night a Father's blessing. Grant to me the sleep which Thou givest to Thy beloved. Or, if I lie wakeful on my bed, may my thoughts of Thee be sweet. Teach me to feel the joy of Thy abiding presence; and in my darkest hour be Thou with me; let Thy rod and Thy staff comfort me.

Thanks be unto Thee, O Lord, for all Thy many mercies. Help me to praise Thee for Thy great goodness, and accept these my prayers for Thy dear Son's sake. Amen.

Our Father, &c.

Thursday Morning.

O MY God, at the beginning of another day I desire to present myself before Thee. Be Thou my Guide, my Director, and my Companion, during every hour of it. May this day be begun, continued, and ended in Thee. Be Thou continually by my side, upholding me, strengthening me, and keeping me from all evil.

O Lord, I acknowledge with sorrow and shame how poorly my past days have been spent. Much precious time has been wasted, never to be recalled. Many things have been left undone, which might have been accomplished. And O how much hast Thou seen that is actually sinful in my daily life.

O my Father, I grieve over the past; I

mourn over my many transgressions, my sins of thought, word, and deed. Thou knowest all. Thou lookest into my very heart; and from Thee no secrets are hid. The remembrance of my sins is grievous unto me, the burden of them is intolerable. Except Thou forgive me, I am lost.

O Saviour, I come to Thy cross as my only refuge. Wash me in Thy most precious blood, and make clean my heart within me. Not only pardon me, Lord, but give me grace to go and sin no more. Enable me to live a holy life. Sanctify me by Thy Holy Spirit. Make my heart pure within. Let no vain thoughts lodge there. Keep from me every unholy desire; and may it be my delight to do Thy will, and to walk in Thy ways.

Lord, I know not what is before me this day, but Thou knowest. I desire to leave all in Thy hands, and to place myself at Thy disposal. Do for me as Thou seest best.

Prosper me in all that I undertake. Give me good success, if such be Thy will. But if Thou seest that crosses and disappointments are better for me, give me grace to accept them as from Thee. Enable me to bear them meekly and cheerfully, and to say, Father, not my will, but Thy will be done.

O my God, make me happy this day in Thy service. Keep my conscience void of offence. Let me do nothing, say nothing, desire nothing, which is contrary to Thy will. Give me a thankful spirit. O for a heart to praise Thee for all that Thou hast given me, and all that Thou hast withheld from me! How glorious Thou art in Thyself, how pure, how holy, how wise, how gracious! And how kind Thou hast been to me, who have so little deserved Thy love! Quicken, I entreat Thee, my sluggish heart to praise Thee now; and grant that I may one day join the heavenly choir, and praise Thee more perfectly with angels and archangels in Thy courts above.

Hear me, O Lord, and do for me abundantly above all I can ask or desire, for the sake of Jesus Christ, my Advocate and Redeemer. Amen.

Our Father, &c.

Thursday Evening.

O MY Saviour, accept me, as I come to
Thee this evening, and put myself under
Thy special care and keeping. Thou art my
best and dearest Friend, my Almighty Pro-
tector, my great Deliverer. In Thy hands
alone I am safe. If Thou dost leave me, I
am destitute. If Thine arm is removed from
me, I have no support.

Saviour, abide with me, I beseech Thee.
Keep me under the shelter of Thy wings this
night, and give me to enjoy that calm and
blessed peace which is the portion of Thy
people. O remove every doubt and every fear
which harass me, and enable me to rejoice in
Thy love and favour. Draw very near to me,
I beseech Thee. Make Thyself more fully

known to me. O that I may walk with Thee all the day, and lie down at night, under Thy peaceful, loving care.

Lord, give me such a portion in this life as is good for me. Grant me health, if it be Thy will. But if Thou shouldest see fit to send me sickness or suffering, give me grace not only to bear it patiently, but to welcome it as sent by Thee. If riches come to me, keep me humble and unworldly; if poverty, make me cheerful and trustful. Whatever be my lot, give me a contented and submissive spirit.

Keep me from being ashamed of Christ, or of His gospel. Give me grace boldly to confess my Saviour before men. And, when my heart faints within me, be Thou the strength of my heart and my portion for ever.

Be with all my beloved friends. Give them earthly happiness, if Thou seest it good for them; and grant them that peace which comes from Thee alone. If any of them are far from Thee, bring them to Thyself (especially ——). If any of them are at this time in trouble, visit them with Thine own presence, and turn their sorrow into joy. Make them to taste of Thy love, and to be happy in Thy service.

Hear me, both for myself and them. And receive me, O my Saviour, now and evermore, for Thine own name's sake. Amen.

Our Father, &c.

Friday Morning.

O THOU, whose name is Love, who never turnest away from the cry of Thy needy children, give ear to my prayer this morning. I dare not enter upon the events of another day without commending my body to Thy protecting care, and my soul to Thy safe keeping.

Make this a day of blessing to me, and make me a blessing to others. Keep all evil away from me. Preserve me from outward transgression, and from secret sin. O Holy Spirit, dwell Thou in my heart. Take up Thy abode within me, and bless me with Thy presence. Teach me, guide me, sanctify me. Draw my soul to the Saviour, and enable me to rest peacefully in Him. My heart is prone to unbelief; O give me faith. It is full of the world; O purify it, and raise my affections heavenwards.

O God, help me to control my temper. May I check the first risings of anger or sullenness. If I meet with unkindness or ill-treatment, give me that charity which suffereth long, and beareth all things. If I am treated wrongfully, may I endure it with patience and meekness, remembering that Thou, my Lord and Master, didst suffer before me. Give me grace to deny myself, to take up my cross, and to follow Thee. Make me kind and gentle towards all, loving even those who love me not.

Lord, let me live this day as if it were to be my last. Keep me from wasting its precious hours, remembering that my time is short. O my God, show me the path that Thou wouldest have me to follow. May I take no step which is not ordered by Thee; and go nowhere except Thou, Lord, go with me.

Holy Father, let Thy will be done concerning

D

me. Let Thy purpose be accomplished. And, if it should be Thy pleasure, use me as an instrument to promote Thy glory, and to be useful to my fellow-men.

Bless to me the reading of Thy word. Be Thou, O Holy Spirit, my daily Teacher. Open to me the hidden things of God. Light up the page of Scripture, and enable me to understand its truths, to believe them, and to rejoice in them.

Lord, hasten Thine own kingdom. Let Thy truth at length triumph. Bless the preaching of Thy gospel in this and other lands. Send forth labourers into Thy harvest. O gather in, and save many souls.

And save me, O Lord, who am now kneeling before Thee. Save me now, and save me throughout eternity, for Jesus Christ's sake. Amen.

Our Father, &c.

Friday Evening.

UNTO Thee do I lift up mine eyes, O Thou that dwellest in the heavens. Thou art great and glorious, but I am vile and worthless. Thou art holy, but I am unholy. Forbid it, Lord, that I should ever come into Thy presence, trusting in my own righteousness; but teach me to come before Thee as a sinner, pleading the merits of my Saviour.

Teach me to pray. O Holy Spirit, help my infirmities, and make me to feel my many and pressing wants. Saviour, I cry to Thee for the pardon of my sins. Enable me to feel their greatness. Let sin appear exceeding sinful in my sight. O deliver me both from its guilt and from its indwelling power. Free me from its dominion; and reign Thou, O my King and my God, reign Thou alone in my heart.

Lord, I wish to be Thine, Thy true servant, Thy faithful disciple. O make me to be so. Correct in me all that is wrong. Take away every branch that beareth not fruit, and may I live to Thee. Pardon all my hateful unbelief, my hardness of heart, and my contempt of Thy blessed word. Forgive me for sometimes doubting Thy love and Thy goodness. Lord, increase my faith. Grant that my trust in Christ may be firm and unshaken. Hast Thou not said, Blessed are they that have not seen, and yet have believed? May that blessedness be mine.

Especially when I read Thy word, or hear it preached, may I receive it as from Thee, as Thy own word, as Thy message to my soul.

Enable me, heavenly Father, to live as a stranger and a pilgrim upon earth, remembering that here I have no abiding city, no resting-place in this world. Grant that I may be ever hastening onward to my home above.

Give me boldness to confess Christ. Let me not be ashamed to own Him as my Master. May I set my face heavenward, and declare plainly that I seek a better country, that is, an heavenly. Loosen those roots which bind me down too closely to this world, and give me grace to press forward with increased earnestness.

I thank Thee, gracious God, for having watched over me and guarded me this day. And I beseech Thee still to keep me under Thy protection. Help me day by day to walk in the narrow path of life. Lead me in the way of holiness, and prayer, and praise, to that glorious kingdom above, where saints and angels bless Thy name for ever.

Grant this, and all that I have asked, or failed to ask, through the merits and intercession of my Lord and Saviour, Jesus Christ. Amen.

Our Father, &c.

Saturday Morning.

O THOU who dwellest in the highest heavens, look down with compassion upon me, Thy sinful creature. Lord, I am unworthy to approach Thee, but I come in the name of Thy dear Son; hear me, for His sake.

Be with me through the whole of this day, in my going out and coming in, in my rising up and lying down. Be with me in my intercourse with my fellow-men. Make me careful as to what I say and do. Let me speak when I ought to speak, and when I should be silent set Thy seal upon my lips.

Be with me also when I am alone. Make me to remember that Thou, O God, seest me; and may I act as in Thy presence. If temptation assail me, O give me grace to resist it.

Shield me, O my God, from the tempter's power, and keep me from sinning against Thee.

O my Father, bless me, and make me a blessing. May my conduct be such as becometh Thy servant and Thy child. May religion be a reality with me. May it be my stay in trouble, my support through life, and the very joy of my heart. Make me not only a Christian, but a holy, happy, rejoicing Christian. Give me that best of all knowledge, to know Thee, the only true God, and Jesus Christ whom Thou hast sent.

As I pass through this world, make me useful. Give me grace to bring forth fruit unto Thee, and to be active, earnest, and zealous in my calling.

Bless the Church to which I belong, and make me a true and faithful member of it. Be with the bishops and pastors of Thy flock; give them wisdom, and piety, and singleness of heart. Clothe Thy ministers with righteousness. O Thou great and good Shepherd, be with those whom Thou sendest forth, and enable them faithfully to feed the flocks committed to their care.

Let Thy blessing also rest upon every member of our Church, especially those with whom I worship. Add to their number daily such as shall be saved. Give life to our souls, and shed abroad Thy love in our hearts.

Be with those also who belong not to our communion. Take away from us all anger and bitterness of heart, and make us to feel a kind and tender spirit towards them. Heal, O Lord, our unhappy divisions, and make us more united. Hasten the time when we shall be one fold, under one Shepherd.

Keep me from thinking evil, or speaking evil of any one this day. Make me slow to discern the faults of others, and quick in discovering my own. May I be anxious to relieve the needy, to cheer the sorrowing, and to return good for evil. May I be ever ready to forgive, hoping to be forgiven of Thee.

Lord, hear me, and bless me, and be with me, for my Saviour's sake. Amen.

Our Father, &c.

Saturday Evening.

O THOU who art my Father and my Friend, who hast watched over me during my past life, and preserved me to this present hour, I desire to thank Thee for that love and mercy which have followed me all my life long.

I bless Thee for all that Thou hast given me, and for all that Thou hast taken from me; for all my trials and sorrows, as well as for all my joys. Thou hast mercifully led me through this wilderness, and hast borne with my many short-comings and evil doings. Thou art indeed most gracious and glorious, a Father of mercies, and a God of love. Rouse this sluggish heart of mine, and fill it with gratitude. Put a new song in my mouth, even thanksgiving unto my God.

And be with me, Lord, for the time to come. I know not what is before me, but Thou knowest. Choose Thou my portion for me. Lead me by Thine own hand; and keep me close to Thee day by day, and night by night. Leave me not for a single instant, lest I fall; but hold Thou me up, and I shall be safe.

My Father, I wish to love and obey Thee. My Saviour, I desire to serve Thee. Take my heart, for I cannot give it to Thee. Put away everything that hinders me from being altogether Thine; and, if need be, loosen every tie that binds me too closely to this world. May I soar upwards on the wings of faith. Grant that the life which I now live in the flesh I may live by the faith of the Son of God, who loved me, and gave Himself for me.

Prepare me, O Lord, for the coming Sabbath-day. Grant that I may not only put aside my worldly occupations, but also my worldly thoughts and feelings. Grant that I may spend its sacred hours in a way that shall conduce to Thy glory, and to my own good. Give me a prayerful and devout frame, and may I lift up my heart to Thee. Be with Thy ministers, and fit them for their holy work.

Lord, I commend to Thy kind and fatherly care all my dear relations and friends. May they be very dear to Thee. Gather every member of my family into Thy fold now, and into Thy kingdom hereafter. Save the lost, bring back the wandering, and make the sorrowful to rejoice.

And now, O Thou Keeper of Israel, keep me. Watch over me whilst I am asleep; or, if I lie awake, help me to think of Thee. And grant me such quiet rest as shall fit me for the duties of the morrow.

Hear me, O my Father, and bless me, for Jesus Christ's sake. Amen.

Our Father, &c.

A Mid-day Prayer.

No. I.

LORD, I desire to withdraw for a while from my earthly occupations, and to spend it in Thy presence. It is good to hold communion with Thee.

O my God, how much the things of earth chain down my soul! Do Thou loose these bonds, and set me free. Raise me above the world; and enable me to live upon Thee, and to walk by faith, and not by sight.

Whilst I am in the world, keep me from its snares. Let me perform my daily work as for Thee. Let mine eye ever be towards Thee. Let me do everything with a view to Thy glory.

Keep me in a watchful, prayerful spirit; and let me never forget that for all I do I must one day give an account to Thee.

Hear me, O my God, for the sake of Jesus Christ, my Redeemer. Amen.

A Mid-day Prayer.

No. II.

HEAR me, O my Saviour, whilst for a few moments I put myself in Thy presence. Make me to feel that Thou lovest me with an everlasting love, and hast given Thyself for me. O that Thy love may possess my heart all the day long! May it constrain me to live no longer to myself, but to Thee. Saviour, hide me in Thy bosom. Keep me by Thy grace, and place beneath me Thine everlasting arms.

Lord, preserve me from the many temptations by which I am surrounded every hour of the day. Keep me close to Thee. Cheer me, strengthen me, and breathe life into my soul. Give me the peace which Thou hast promised to Thy people, even that peace which the world cannot give. For Thine own sake, O Lord, grant this my prayer. Amen.

A Mid-day Prayer.

No. III.

O MY God, enable me to retire from my earthly calling, to spend a few short moments with Thee. Jesus, look graciously upon me. Pardon me for being so taken up with this present world, that I too often forget Thee. Take Thou fuller possession of my heart. Set up Thy throne within me, and draw all my affections to Thyself. May I often think of Thee in the midst of my necessary employments.

O my Saviour, choose Thou my path for me, and keep me every moment by Thy almighty grace. When I am ready to fall, do Thou uphold me. If at any time I should be disposed to take a wrong step, do Thou check me. If I should be cast down, comfort me and strengthen me. When alone, make

me watchful : when with others, make me
kind, gentle, and loving.

Be Thou my Helper, my Guide, my never-
failing Support, both now and evermore.
Amen.

A Prayer before receiving the Holy Communion.

O THOU high and holy One, who hast prepared a table for me in the wilderness, and invitest me to partake of the Feast which Thou hast spread, help me to approach Thee in that holy sacrament with a penitent, believing, loving heart.

O my Saviour, Thou who art the Bread of Life, nourish my soul, for it needs Thy constant support. Give me right feelings in coming to Thy table. Put away from me all worldliness, and sin, and unbelief. Purify my heart. Fill me with love to Thee. I look to Thy cross for pardon, and to Thy Holy Spirit for sanctifying grace. I look to Thee as my great Helper, as my ever-present Lord and Friend.

Be with me now especially. Manifest Thyself to me in the breaking of bread. Draw nearer to me than Thou hast ever yet done, and make me to feel joy and comfort in this Thine own ordinance. Bring me to Thy banqueting-house, and may Thy banner over me be love.

O bless me, strengthen me, feed me, refresh me, both now and evermore. Amen.

Our Father, &c.

E

A Prayer to be used under Spiritual Doubts and Difficulties.

O THOU who art my Guide and Friend, my Counsellor, and my Support, to Thee I come in this my time of need. Lord, Thou knowest how sorely I am tried by spiritual doubts and fears. Háve compassion on me. Pity Thy poor, weak servant; and in Thy own good time make every difficulty to vanish.

In the meanwhile support me by Thy grace. Hold Thou me up, lest I sink. Let not the waves overwhelm me. Speak to my heart, and make me to feel Thy love towards me. Show me that Thou art indeed my Father. Lord, I believe : help Thou mine unbelief.

Remove every cloud that now darkens my soul; and shine upon me, O Thou Sun of Righteousness, with healing in Thy wings.

Take away all that hinders me from enjoying peace, and restore unto me the joy of Thy salvation. Give me grace to cast myself unreservedly on Thee, who art my Saviour and my Friend; and to Thee be all the praise, now and for evermore. Amen.

Our Father, &c.

𝔄 𝔓rayer for any 𝔗ime of 𝔗emptation.

O MY God, at this time, when temptation presses sore upon me, I flee unto Thee for help. O Thou most mighty One, come to my deliverance.

Thou hast bidden me resist the devil; but I have no power to do so, except it be given me from above. Thou knowest my weakness and my danger; help me, I entreat Thee. Strengthen me, uphold me, fill me with Thy grace. Saviour, let Thy strength be made perfect in my weakness. And when Satan would have me, and sift me as wheat, do Thou pray for me, that I may manfully fight against him, and at length gain the victory.

Lord Jesus, who wast Thyself tempted, and who lovest to succour them that are tempted, deliver me, I beseech Thee. Stand by me in my hour of need ; and keep me from falling into any sin, or doing anything that will dishonour Thee.

Hearken to Thy servant in his distress; and when Thou hearest, put forth Thy power to save, for Thy own sake, who, with the Father and the Holy Ghost, art God over all, blessed for evermore. Amen.

Our Father, &c.

𝔄 𝔓𝔯𝔞𝔶𝔢𝔯 𝔱𝔬 𝔟𝔢 𝔲𝔰𝔢𝔡 𝔦𝔫 𝔗𝔦𝔪𝔢 𝔬𝔣 𝔖𝔦𝔠𝔨𝔫𝔢𝔰𝔰.

MOST gracious and loving Father, I thank Thee for the measure of health which I have hitherto enjoyed, for having preserved me up to the present hour, and for all the many mercies which I have experienced.

And now that Thou hast brought sickness upon me, I desire still to thank Thee ; for that also cometh from Thee. It is for my good that Thou layest Thy chastening hand upon me. O grant that I may profit by this Thy visitation. Make me to feel that I am in Thy hands, and that Thou canst take away my health, my strength, and my life. I bow before Thee with humble submission. Father, not my will, but Thine be done.

If it be Thy pleasure, remove this sickness

from me, and restore me again to health. Or if it be Thy purpose to keep me on a bed of sickness, sanctify this affliction to my soul's health. May it do me good. May it wean me from the world. I feel that I have been too much engrossed with the things of time; O that I may think more of eternity!

Whatever be Thy dealings with me at this time, leave me not, O Lord, neither forsake me. Draw near to me, and bless me with Thy presence. Enable me to rest my soul on Christ, and keep me in perfect peace.

Hear me, and receive me, for my Saviour's sake. Amen.

Our Father, &c.

A Prayer on Recovery from Sickness.

O MY God, I desire to bless and praise Thee for Thy unspeakable mercy in thus restoring me to health. In the time of sickness Thou wast indeed most gracious to me. Thy chastening hand was upon me; but it was a hand of love. Thou didst call me aside for a while, that I might trim my lamp, and set my house in order. Thanks be to Thee for dealing so lovingly with me.

Grant that this visitation may never be forgotten by me. May it have left many a blessing behind it. O that my future course may be marked by more devotedness to my Saviour, more humility, more love, and more earnestness of heart and life. I desire now solemnly to dedicate myself to Thy more immediate service.

O Holy Spirit, deepen Thy work in my soul. Sanctify me wholly, so that I may be more entirely Thine than I have ever yet been. Yea, Lord, take up Thine abode within me; and comfort me with Thine indwelling presence. May I become a faithful and decided Christian, and live from henceforth only to Thy glory.

Grant this, O heavenly Father, for Jesus Christ's sake. Amen.

Our Father, &c.

A Prayer to be used in Time of Prosperity.

O MY Father, Thou hast indeed blest me far beyond my deserts. Thou hast greatly prospered me. O make me thankful. Tune my heart to praise Thee as I ought. Put a new song in my mouth, even thanksgiving unto my God.

Keep me from being too much taken up with the things of this world. Make me ever mindful that this is not my rest. I desire to show my gratitude by living henceforth more entirely to Thy glory. Let me not forget Thee in my present prosperity, lest a curse come upon me instead of a blessing. But feeling Thy goodness and Thy love, may I give my whole heart to Thee, and live to Thee all my days, for Jesus Christ's sake. Amen.

Our Father, &c.

A Prayer to be used in Time of Adversity.

O GOD, to Thee alone I trust in this hour of affliction. Thou hast sorely smitten me, but it is in love to my soul.

Thou pitiest me, O my Father, and wilt not lay upon me a burden too heavy for me to bear. May I find abundant support from Thee. Place under me Thine everlasting arms; and make me to feel that as my days so shall my strength be. Enable me to come out of this furnace purified. Saviour, I flee to Thee. Hide me under the covert of Thy wings, and speak peace to my soul. I do not ask Thee to take away my sorrow before the appointed time; but I ask Thee to be with me in it. And after I have suffered awhile, stablish, strengthen, settle me.

Hear me at this time; and send me not away unblest from Thy Throne of grace. Amen.

Our Father, &c.

A Prayer before Reading the Bible.

O LORD, Thy word is before me; give me a meek, and reverent, and teachable frame whilst I read it. Open to me its sacred truths, and enable me to receive it, not as the word of men, but as the word of God which liveth and abideth for ever.

Be Thou, O blessed Spirit, my Teacher. Enlighten my mind, and prepare my heart. Shine, Lord, upon Thy own sacred page, and make it clear to me. What I see not, show me; and where I am wrong, correct me. Bring home some precious portion to my soul, and thus make me wise unto salvation, through Jesus Christ, my Saviour. Amen.

Our Father, &c.

A Prayer to be used before any Special Undertaking.

LORD, I desire to place myself, and what I am about to undertake, in Thy hands. Guide, direct, and prosper me, I beseech Thee. And if Thou seest that this undertaking will be for Thy glory, grant me good success. Make me, and those who act with me, to feel that unless Thy blessing is with us we cannot succeed, and that except the Lord build the house, their labour is but lost that build it. Prevent us then, O Lord, in this and all our doings with Thy most gracious favour, and further us with Thy continual help, that in all our works begun, continued, and ended in Thee, we may glorify Thy name, through Jesus Christ. Amen.

Our Father, &c.

A Prayer for a Blessing on Christ's Ministers.

MOST blessed Saviour, who hast appointed divers orders of men in Thy Church, look graciously at this time upon Thy ministering servants. Endue them with Thy Holy Spirit. Make them apt to teach, gentle to persuade, and wise to win souls. Cheer and comfort them in their labours. Feed them with that bread of life which they deal out to their people. Bless them in their labours, and make them willing to spend and be spent for Thee.

Lord Jesus, let Thine especial favour rest upon those who are preaching Thy gospel to the heathen. Support them amidst all their trials; and grant that the word spoken by their mouths may have such success, that it may never be spoken in vain.

And hasten, Lord, the time when they shall no more teach every man his neighbour, and every man his brother, saying, Know the Lord ; for all shall know Thee, from the least to the greatest. Grant this for Thine own name's sake. Amen.

Our Father, &c.

HEADS FOR PRAYER.

Morning Prayer.

SUNDAY.

CONFESSION .. Coldness in prayer. Abuse of past
sabbaths.

PETITION .... For God's presence. Gift of the Spirit
to ministers and congregations. The
awakening and nourishing of souls.

PRAISE ...... For day of rest. Public worship. An
ordained ministry.

MONDAY.

CONFESSION .. Hardness and dulness of heart. Sloth-
fulness.

PETITION .... For Jews. Heathens. Our own coun-
trymen.

PRAISE ...... For Gospel light. Prayer. Christ's
intercession.

TUESDAY.

CONFESSION .. Vain thoughts. Idle words. Unholy
tempers.

PETITION .... For Patience. Forbearance. A blessing on the sick, sorrowful, aged,
young.

PRAISE ...... For Health. Sleep. Food. Clothing.
Safety. Opportunities of doing good.

WEDNESDAY.

CONFESSION .. Bible neglected. Heaven not kept in
view. Love of the world.

PETITION .... For influence of the Holy Spirit. A
kinder and gentler feeling towards all.

PRAISE ...... For any good in ourselves or others.
Grace received.

THURSDAY.

CONFESSION .. Unhumbled mind. Hasty words. Un-
charitable thoughts.

PETITION .... For a blessing on our Country; our
Queen; all in authority; the poor;
our enemies.

PRAISE ...... For the gift of a Saviour. Pardoning,
restraining, and sanctifying grace.

FRIDAY.

CONFESSION .. Want of kindness and tenderness. Self-
seeking. Self-indulgence.

PETITION .... For Family. Friends. Parish. God-
children.

PRAISE ...... For the Spirit's teaching. Prosperity.
Trials.

SATURDAY.

CONFESSION .. Selfishness. Jealousy. Fretfulness.
Love of Praise.

PETITION .... For our Church. Bishops and Ministers. A desire to promote God's
glory.

PRAISE ...... For our Home. Family blessings.
Kind friends.

F

Evening Prayer.

SUNDAY.

CONFESSION .. Wanderings of thought. Iniquity of
our holy things. Unbelief. Uncon-
cern.
PETITION .... For a blessing on the seed sown. More
life and earnestness.
PRAISE ...... For Sabbath mercies. God's forbearance. For a Saviour offered to us.

MONDAY.

CONFESSION .. Indwelling sin. Backwardness to confess Christ.
PETITION .... For a consistent walk. Communion
with God. More faith.
PRAISE ...... For temporal mercies. God's love.

TUESDAY.

CONFESSION .. Our lost state by nature. Unwatch-
fulness. Self-esteem.
PETITION .... To be useful. More love for souls.
PRAISE ...... For our privileges. For God's chas-
tisements. For common mercies.

WEDNESDAY.

CONFESSION .. Readiness to take offence. Sinful de-
　　　　　　　sires.
PETITION .... That Christ would make Himself known
　　　　　　　to us. A holy walk.
PRAISE ...... For our reason.　Deliverance from
　　　　　　　danger, and from evil.

THURSDAY.

CONFESSION .. Duties neglected. Grieving the Spirit.
PETITION .... To live a life of faith. Power to resist
　　　　　　　the devil.
PRAISE ...... For sparing mercy. For our promised
　　　　　　　rest.

FRIDAY.

CONFESSION .. Lost time and opportunities. Worldli-
　　　　　　　ness of heart.
PETITION .... For growth in grace and holiness. A
　　　　　　　contented and thankful heart. God's
　　　　　　　protecting care.
PRAISE ...... For answered prayers. The promise of
　　　　　　　Christ's Second Coming.

SATURDAY.

CONFESSION .. Self-indulgence. Love of ease. Love
　　　　　　　of money.
PETITION .... For the outpouring of the Spirit. A
　　　　　　　blessing on the morrow.
PRAISE ...... For God's care. His patience and love.

www.ingramcontent.com/pod-product-compliance
Lightning Source LLC
Chambersburg PA
CBHW022150090426
42742CB00010B/1453